MW01383802

CONTENTS

ILLINOIS GOVERNOR EDWARD COLES (1822-1826)

BIOGRAPHY

Mary D. Hébert

Edward Coles ashes are not mixed with Illinois soil. His dedication, suffering, and voice for freedom will be with Illinois for eternity.

INTRODUCTION

E dward Coles knew that slavery was wrong. Governor Coles led Illinois in passing a law against slavery. He also set an example by freeing his inherited slaves and giving them a place to live.

I struggled to understand the deep-seated slavery issues in Illinois. It goes back to the French settlers in the early 1700's. I learned in school that Illinois was a free state and Missouri was a slave state. I wrote several history books for the United States Air Force. I was active duty during the post-Vietnam War and the Gulf War. Those proprietary books were about the issue, what solved the issue, and did we win. If we win it's a war. If we lose it's an era or campaign. There were no arguments to present.

Later, I looked at political history issues with a more personal investment. I wondered what were the people like? Where did they live? What mattered to them? This led to a more social history point of view.

I've lived in Illinois for 30 years and never heard of Governor Edward Coles. The only thing named after him is Coles County. There is a Coles monument in Edwardsville. Coles freed his slaves and passed legislation to abolish slavery. It took Illinois another 40 years to abolish indentured servitude even though it was against the law. President Abraham Lincoln passed the Emancipation Proclamation 1864.

Why does any of this matter to me? It does because Illinois is unique. Especially Southern Illinois. I can drive down to Fort de Chartres but I don't see slaves there. I don't hear much about them. Historians know about slaves. That is because slavery was part of the Illinois fabric since the Eighteenth Century. I take you on a short journey not to present an argument. Not to point out problems. I take you on a road that explains Edward Coles' point of view through the documents he wrote. I answer how he felt about slavery. How he came to believe that all men were created equal and free!

The issue of slavery caused the Civil War in 1861. It was a dangerous time for people living in Illinois. I'm impressed that against all odds, Edward Coles lost everything he had to prove that all men are equal and free. He saw that Illinois could be the land of the free. It opened the door for other Northwest Territories to become free states.

You have a sense that there is good among the bad. Coles enlisted many men to help him spread the word of freedom. Communication was done by letters, news print, and travelling. One of those travelers was Reverend John Mason Peck. He spread the news of freedom to Southern Illinois. Peck knew that education would be essential for early Illinois to survive. He started the first college in Illinois. Public schools were started as Illinois grew in numbers.

This is a part of history that lurks behind the shadow of Abraham Lincoln. Abraham Lincoln is bigger than life in Illinois. The history of Illinois goes much deeper. You will walk away from this book with a better sense of Illinois history. Rural Illinois is proud of its heritage. Coles lived in Edwardsville. It was beautiful land near the Mississippi River. He found that Illinois was not all prairie. There was flat farmland surrounded by hills lined with trees for protection. Creeks and rivers were plenty. Coles knew he wanted to live here and knew it was good for settlers. As you turn the pages you will see yourself in Coles shoes. Enjoy the journey!

CHAPTER ONE

*Early Years Shaping Coles
for Leadership*

G overnor Edward Coles was a man ahead of his time. He formed his early ideas about anti-slavery at William and Mary College in Virginia. His grandfather and his father owned a plantation in Virginia. Their neighbors were Thomas Jefferson, James Monroe, and James Madison. Edward Coles would inherit the plantation along with the slaves. This made Coles sad because he thought slavery was a curse on America. How could all men be free if some men were not? In 1819, Coles brought his inherited slaves to Edwardsville, Illinois and freed them. This was against all tradition and there was no man who had done this. It made him go from rich to poor. He knew he had a duty to his Providence. His heart was always to free his slaves. The slaves always knew he would free them some day. They were surprised when it happened so early in their lives. Most of the slaves were under 30 years old and some of those had their families with them and some were single. Coles bought each family 160 acres of land to use as collateral after they got established. Coles ran for governor in 1822 with the sole purpose of making Illinois a free state. This would be four decades before Abraham Lincoln signed the Emancipation Proclamation.

It is impossible to talk about Edward Coles without talking about what shaped his life. His early years resulted in his ability to be successful. Colonel John Coles II (1745–1808) and Rebecca Elizabeth Tucker had Edward Coles. He was born on December 15th, 1786 in Albemarle County, Virginia. They had 13 children, 10 of them lived to adulthood, and Edward was the youngest child. Colonel John Coles II served in the Revolutionary War. He inherited the beautiful estate called "Enniscorthy". Edward Coles' grandfather was John Coles (1705–1747). He immigrated from Enniscorthy, County Wexford, Ireland in 1730. Coles grandfather lived in Richmond, Virginia for a time. Then settled his plantation in

Virginia which was next to Thomas Jefferson's Monticello, James Monroe's Ash Lawn, and James Madison's Montpelier.

Young Edward Coles

We know that Coles was taught at home by private tutors to prepare him for college. He attended Hampden-Sydney College for one semester. Then transferred to the College of William and Mary during the Autumn of 1805. This college helped shape Coles ideas about all American's deserve to be free. He engaged in a series of discussions with the Reverend James Madison. Madison was an Episcopal Bishop and the college president. Madison and Coles discussed the Bible, enlightenment ideals, and republican theories of government. He was pleased with the progress that Coles was making.

On June 25, 1807, Coles left college without graduating to go home. While Coles was at his plantation home in Virginia his father, John Coles II, died in the winter of 1808. Cole was now 23 years old and the owner of a plantation and approximately 19 slaves. Because Cole had formed his ideas early in his college day's he knew he would free his slaves. He did not tell his family right away because they would oppose his decision.

By now, Edward Coles was a distinguished gentleman from a wealthy family. He had a privileged education and he appeared handsome. He had a reputation that made his family proud of him. Remember when Coles father would entertain notable men like James Madison? Well, President James Madison took notice of Coles. He asked Coles to be his personal secretary. This was a prestigious position in the house of the president. At first, Coles was going to turn down his offer but his friend, James Monroe, encouraged him to take it. Coles was in the position by the end of January 1810.

Coles tried to talk to Thomas Jefferson. He wrote a series of letters to his friend and neighbor in 1814. He encouraged Jefferson to join in manumitting (or freeing) his slaves. Jefferson declined. He reminded Coles that freedom might mean hardship for former slaves. They would be required to leave Virginia within one year.

Coles plans to free his slaves were interrupted. President James Madison asked Coles to go on a diplomatic mission to Russia. There was a sensitive diplomatic argument going on between Russia and America. In the summer of 1816, Coles set out from Boston Harbor. He sailed east across the Atlantic Ocean and entered the Baltic Sea on a U.S. man-of-war, the Prometheus. In St. Petersburg, he was kept waiting three months for the emperor of Russia. Emperor Alexander was traveling in Moscow and Poland.

When the emperor returned, Coles negotiating skills allowed him to resolve the problem. Coles would spend some time travelling in Europe before he returned to America.

After being abroad for a year, Edward Coles second appearance in Illinois was at Kaskaskia in 1818. This was the government seat in the Illinois Territory. He lingered here for several weeks. He found out that they were writing the constitution for the new State of Illinois. Coles sold his Virginia real estate to his older brother, Walter. At this point, he decided to return to Virginia and brought his slaves to Illinois with the plan to free them.

Edward Coles Manumitting His Free People

On April 1st, 1819, Edwards left his plantation called the Rock-fish. He had all his 'negroes' except two women that were in old age. The women were part of two families who belonged to Edward's mother. Coles supported them for the rest of their lives. The slaves knew they were leaving Virginia and going to the Northwest Territory. They did not know that Coles would free them.

He directed his slaves to set out from the plantation, heading north then west. Coles travelled alone on a horse. The group of slaves met Coles at Brownsville, Pennsylvania, and they were put on two boats. They floated along the Ohio River heading west. Ohio was the boundary where the free states started.

The following description was the most important decision to manumit his slaves. Many men of great wealth and position did not free their slaves. Coles was stepping out in uncharted territory. He risked losing extended family, wealth, position, influential friends, and everything he enjoyed. The underlying stench of human slavery and its curse on society was frightening to Coles. This sentiment spurred Coles' to make his slaves free men.

This was transcribed from Edward Coles own handwriting about freeing his slaves: *"The morning after we left Pittsburg, a mild, calm and lovely April day, the sun shining bright, and the heavens without a cloud, our boats floating gently down the beautiful Ohio, the verdant foliage of Spring just budding out on its picturesque banks, all around presenting a scene both conducive to and in harmony with the finest feelings of our nature, was selected as one well suited to make known to my negroes the glad tidings of their freedom. Being curious to see the effect of an instantaneous severing of the manacles of bondage, and letting loose on the buoyant wings of liberty the long pent up spirit of man, I called on the deck of the boats, which were lashed together, all the negroes, and made them a short address, in which I commenced by saying it was time for me to make known to them what I intended to do with them, and concluded my remarks by so expressing myself, that by a turn of a sentence, I proclaimed in the shortest and fullest manner possible, that they were no longer slaves, but free—free as I was, and were at liberty to proceed with me, or to go ashore at their pleasure.*

The effect on them was electrical. They stared at me and at each other, as if doubting the accuracy or reality of what they "heard. In breathless silence, they stood before me, unable to utter a word, but with countenances beaming with expression which no words could convey, and which no language can now describe. As they began to see the truth of what they had heard, and to realize their situation, there came on a kind of hysterical, giggling laugh. After a pause of intense an unutter-

able emotion, bathed in tears, and with tremulous voices, they gave vent to their gratitude, and implored the blessings of God on me. When they had in some degree recovered the command of themselves, Ralph said he had long known I was opposed to holding black people as slaves, and thought it probable I would some time or other give my people their freedom, but that he did not expect me to do it so soon; and moreover, he thought I ought not to do it till they had repaid me the expense I had been at in removing them from Virginia, and had improved my farm and 'gotten me well fixed in that new country'. To this, all simultaneously expressed their concurrence, and their desire to remain with me, as my servants, until they had comfortably fixed me at my new home.

I told them, no. I had made up my mind to give to them immediate and unconditional freedom; that I had long been anxious to do it, but had been prevented by the delays, first in selling my property in Virginia, and then in collecting the money, and by other circumstances. That in consideration of this delay, and as a reward for their past services, as well as a stimulant to their future exertions, and with a hope it would add to their self-esteem and their standing in the estimation of others, I should give to each head of a family a quarter section, containing one hundred and sixty acres of land. To this all objected, saying I had done enough for them in giving them their freedom; and insisted on my keeping the land to supply my own wants, and added, in "the kindest manner, the expression of their solicitude that I would not have the means of doing so after I had freed them. I told them I had thought much of my duty and of their rights, and that it was due alike to both that I should do what I had said I should do; and accordingly, soon after reaching Edwardsville, I executed and delivered to them deeds to the lands promised them.

I stated to them that the lands I intended to give them were unimproved lands, and as they would not have the means of making the necessary improvements, of stocking their farms, and procuring the materials for at once living on them, they would have to hire themselves out till they could acquire by their labor the necessary means to commence cultivating and residing on their own lands. That I was willing to *hire and employ on my farm a certain number of them (designating the individuals;) the others I advised to seek employment in St. Louis, Edwardsville, and other places, where smart, active young men and women could obtain much higher wages than they could on farms. At this some of them murmured, as it indicated a partiality they said, on my part to those designated to live with me; and contended they should all be equally dear to me, and that I ought not to keep a part and turn the others out on the world, to be badly treated, etc. I reminded them of what they seemed to have lost sight of, that they were free; that no one had a right to beat or ill use them; and if so treated, they could at pleasure leave one place and seek a better; that labor was much in demand in that new country, and highly paid for; that there would be no difficulty in their obtaining good places, and being kindly treated; but if not, I should be at hand, and would see they were well treated, and have justice done them.*

I availed myself of the deck scene to give the negroes some advice. I dwelt long and with much earnestness on their future conduct and success, and my great anxiety that they should behave themselves and do well, not only for their own sakes, but for the sake of the black race held in bondage; many of whom were thus held, because their masters believed they were incompetent to take care of themselves, and that liberty would be to them a curse rather than a blessing. My anxious wish was that they should so conduct themselves as to show by their example that the descendants of Africa were competent to take care of and govern themselves, and enjoy all the blessings of liberty, and all the other birth rights of man, and thus promote the universal emancipation of that unfortunate and outraged race of the human family."

Coles had the biggest impact on Illinois history as a free state. It is important to note that Edward Coles only lived in Illinois for about thirteen years. He is almost unknown today. The reason is two-fold. Coles only lived in Illinois 13 years. The other part of this equation is that most of Coles documents were burned in a fire. He collected documents when he was the land register and the governor. Coles gave the documents to his friend who was going to write the History of Illinois. Reverend John Mason Peck's house burned in a fire. The documents were lost in the fire. After Edward Coles death, his son gave his letters to a well-known historian. Elihu Benjamin Washburne, from Illinois wrote the *'Sketch of Edward Coles'*.

CHAPTER TWO

Early Edwardsville in the Middle of Nowhere

E dward Coles lived and owned land in Edwardsville, Illinois. When he was governor he lived in Vandalia and worked at the State House in Vandalia. Let's see what Edwardsville was like during the decade that he freed his slaves and owned a farm.

Edward Coles explains in his own words: "*To show you the state of things when I entered Illinois* [1815], *I was assured at Vincennes that there were no houses of accommodation on the way, and moreover, that it was not safe from Indian massacre, to go from there directly west to St. Louis, but that I would have to go by way of Shawneetown and Kaskaskia. This I did, and passed up from the latter town through the comparatively old and thick French and American settlements up to Madison, then a frontier county which had but recently been laid out, and its seat of justice (Edwardsville) located on Thos. Kirkpatrick's farm. There was but one small log cabin on the site of the old town of Edwardsville, and that having no person in it when I passed, and seeing no marks showing the town had been laid out, I passed on the road over the site without knowing I had done so. At the creek at the north end of the intended county town was a small mill which together with its dam was in such, a dilapidated state as not to admit of its being then used. I passed on through Ratton's prairie, where then resided several fam-*

ilies, to the banks of the Mississippi river, where there was a small improvement made at the outlet of a rivulet on the south of where Alton was afterwards located. I was told there were then but four or five families residing to the north of that. From this point I descended through the American Bottom to St. Louis. After examining the surrounding country, and making a purchase of land, I yielded to a desire I had to see the descent and outlet to the ocean of the country I intended to make my permanent home, and went to New Orleans, and from thence passed on through the seaboard country to my mothers who resided on my native spot in Virginia."

Edwardsville was in Madison County which was organized from St. Clair County in 1812. Coles first visit to Edwardsville was in 1815 when he toured Illinois to see if he could settle there. He found Ohio's and Indiana's people too wild for his taste. He found 750 square miles of land along the Mississippi River near Edwardsville. This had the best land for farming but it was a combination of wooded hills and prairie in the America Bottoms. It was perfect for living, protected from the elements, and showed promise for farming. The water source was provided by Silver Creek and Cahokia Creek. He found that coal and building limestone were abundant. He saw the best timber in Illinois was located around Alton, Wood River [the river not town], and Cahokia Creek.

Fast forward to 1837 which was four years after Coles left Illinois. Coles friend Reverend John Mason Peck, wrote an Illinois gazetteer. He said that Edwardsville's location was pleasant. It was located on high ground, it was fertile, and well-watered. It had matured timbered country and possessed enterprising farmers. Peck's reports that Edwardsville had become the seat of justice for Madison County. It had a court house, jail of brick, two taverns, and a castor oil factory. There were two physicians, four lawyers, various mechanics, and about 70 families. Peck further noted that the Baptists and the Methodists had houses of worship. He saw that the people were industrious, intelligent, and moral. There were a large proportion of professors of religion.

Peck cites that the approximate population of Madison County was 6,640 in 1831. The Illinois census was taken in 1830.

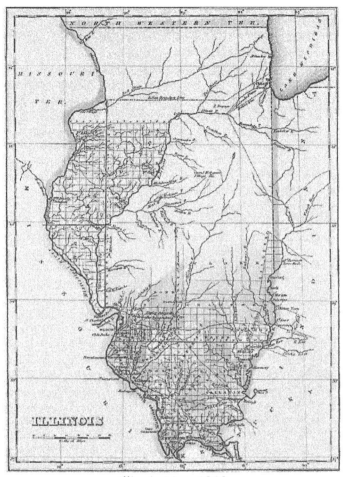

Illinois Map 1818

When Illinois became the twenty first state in 1818, they needed schools for children. In 1825, a law was made that allowed school districts to become incorporated. There were features of the law that were not popular. The legislators soon realized that getting qualified teachers was a problem. There were no requirements for choosing qualified teachers. The teacher did not have to prove that they could teach and they were not interviewed by a competent board. In other words, the law was ineffective without qualified teachers. All the taxes and land sales to pay for the school were not going to fix this. This was a fledgling state with hard working people in their settlements. Their children's common school education was behind the other 20 states. They had to establish rules that insured the teachers were sober, moral, and had teaching experience in return for pay.

The state worked on trying to come up with a good common school system. All was not lost in early education. There were several good primary schools. A good school could come from concerned citizens. Three or four leading families would unite and find a good teacher. Then oversee the success of the school in their settlement. As students progressed in their learning, they needed a college education.

UPPER ALTON: SHURTLEFF COLLEGE.

There were many colleges that existed in Illinois at that time.

The Seminary at Rock Spring was started by Reverend John Mason Peck of Rock Spring, Illinois in 1827. Rock Spring is now O'Fallon, Illinois. It was the first college in Illinois. In 1835, Peck sought funds in the eastern states and $10,000 was donated by Benjamin Shurtleff M.D. of Boston. The Seminary at Rock Spring was moved to Alton, Illinois. It was renamed Shurtleff College. They had about 60 students. Shurtleff College exists today as the Southern Illinois University Dental School at Edwardsville. The Alton Theological Seminary was started. It had a different mission than Shurtleff College. It was taught by a theological professor with seven or eight students. It was supported by Baptist churches. McKendree College in Lebanon, Illinois was established in 1828. It is the oldest surviving college in Illinois today. McKendree College was under the supervision of the Methodist Church. It had 50 students.

CHAPTER THREE

Slaves or Indentured Servants

T he discussion in Missouri about slavery shook Illinois to the core. John Reynolds [4th governor of Illinois] reminisced in this quote: "*The people in Illinois, in 1820, were ready almost to commit violence on one another, and in fact the whole Union [America] was so agitated that, like an earthquake, no one knew when it would subside, and all friends of the integrity of the Union were alarmed and shuddered at the fearful consequence of the agitation, and the sectional feelings produced on the occasion.*"

Let's look at slavery in Illinois history. There was a French military presence at Fort Kaskaskia and Fort de Chartres in the 1700's. Their governing orders came from New Orleans. Travelling and communication was possible by the Mississippi River. It was called the Illinois country and it was a part of the Louisiana Territory owned by France. This was a time when France was interested in owning land in America. This took place before and during the Seven Years War [1756-1763]. The United States bought it from France in 1803 and call it the Louisiana Purchase.

Carl Ekberg, historian, says it this way: "*It is evident that beginning as early as circa 1720, black slaves worked as agricultural laborers in the Illinois Country, and that by the end of the colonial era they were being widely used on both sides of the Mississippi* [River]." Illinois people owned slaves and this was imbedded into the fabric of Illinois. Even the first Governor of Illinois was a slave owner. And this thinking continued into Governor Coles time.

This French ownership of slaves makes Illinois unique. It goes back to the 1720's. The Northwest Ordinance of 1787 prohibited slavery in the Northwest Territory. Curiously, the Illinois territorial laws did not prohibit slavery. So, people kept their slaves. Settlers from the south, brought slaves with them. When land was sold in early Illinois, the slaves were part of that estate. This was an old French law that was adopted in Illinois. Owning slaves continued until the Emancipation Proclamation was signed in 1863. And yes, Governor Coles passed the anti-slavery legislation in 1824. The owners of slaves just called them indentured servants. Some were indentured servants until they died. So, it was still tolerated and remained a blight on humanity.

President Thomas Jefferson could not eliminate slavery in the Northwest Territory in 1784. The Northwest Ordinance of 1787 abolished slavery with a unanimous vote. The sixth article provided that neither slavery nor involuntary servitude shall exist. Jefferson was pleased.

Some owners in Illinois were still deeply invested in slavery. They were resistant to move away from it. This bothered Jefferson. He asked Reverend James Lemen to move to Illinois. His purpose was to establish churches to promote anti-slavery in the new territory. Lemen and his family moved to Illinois in 1787 and Lemen started eight Baptist churches. He was enthusiastic in his anti-slavery sentiments. Some of those churches remained pro-slavery. Lemen influenced the Illinois' first Free State Constitution. It was framed in 1818 and passed in 1824. President Abraham Lincoln would later cite this as a positive move. It led towards the passing of the Illinois anti-slavery legislation.

This summary is a very small picture. It explains the complexity of the Illinois slavery issue. Thus, Governor Coles faced a very difficult task. He had to pass legislation to forbid slavery. This would be important to America. As new states came into the Union, they would be anti-slavery states.

Coles says: "*The next winter I went to the eastward* [Virginia], *and when I returned in the spring, having at last collected my debt, I was enabled to bring with me my colored people, whose expenses I paid, and gave each family a quarter section of land as compensation for the delay in bringing them from Virginia. I hired some of them to work a farm I owned near Edwardsville, the others hired themselves in Illinois and St. Louis.*" Coles never considered his '*colored people*' as property. Otherwise, he would have sold the land and the slaves together as property and made money.

CHAPTER FOUR

Second Governor of Illinois

While Coles was working as a personal secretary for President Madison, he became interested in Illinois. Madison's office was dealing with Indiana and Ohio. This was because of the Northwest Ordinance of 1787. It declared those states as free from slavery. This was attractive to Coles since his goal was to free his slaves that he inherited from his father.

After Coles freed his slaves in 1819, he ran for Governor of Illinois in 1822 and won. It was distressing for Coles to find out that Illinois was still practicing slavery. Governor Coles declared that Illinois needed a better anti-slavery law.

Governor Edward Coles presented his inaugural speech at the Vandalia State House. Both houses of the General Assembly of Illinois were in attendance. His inaugural address focused on internal improvements. There were issues facing the State Bank of Illinois and Coles wanted a return to silver and gold. Farming and education needed laws. A need for a canal to link Lake Michigan with the Illinois River became his concern. He called for an end to slavery in the state.

There was a reaction to this abrupt proposal. A pro-slavery faction in the Illinois legislature called for a constitutional convention. Their overt purpose was to legalize slavery. Not everyone in Illinois was upset about this straight forward speech. The people who wanted a free state were supportive. Such as, Morris Birkbeck, who wrote a letter to Governor Coles on December 21, 1822. *"I should write to you even were it only for the pleasure of telling you that your speech has made a very favorable impression m [on me] this quarter, and is highly commended, both as to matter and composition. Judge Wattles, a New Yorker, a man of talents, says it reminds him of Governor Clinton in good sense and plainness. This, I believe, he considers the maximum of praise."*

Governor Coles won the governor position by 50 votes. There were three other men that were running for governor. One of which was Chief Justice Phillips who was pro-slavery. Many of the pro-slavery people fled their states because they could not hold slaves. This made Illinois their home for keeping their slaves. These men were more pro-slavery than the states they left. They saw Chief Justice Phillips as a way to realize their dreams for Illinois as a slave state. The majority of people that voted in this election were slave holders. They elected pro-slavery politicians in both branches of the legislature for their benefit. They were well organized and saw this as an opportune time to go against Governor Coles.

Remember when Congress passed the Northwest Ordinance? It provided for neither slavery nor involuntary servitude in the Northwestern Territory. There was opposition that this ordinance of 1787 was in conflict with the deed of cession. It no longer had a binding effect. The Union had no way to enforce the laws.

There was another conflict in the laws. Illinois was a slave territory when it was ceded by Virginia to the United States. The deed of cession from Virginia, March 1, 1784, stated that, "... *the inhabitants of the Territory ceded, who professed themselves to have been citizens of Virginia previous to the cession should have their possessions and titles confirmed to them, and be protected in their rights and liberties."* Also, the early 1700's held that French slaveholders had a similar law. One that allowed property and slaves to be sold together. There were two periods that guaranteed the right of French settlers to have slaves. One was the treaty between France and England [1763]. The other was between England and the United States after the Revolutionary War. So, you can see the deep imbedded laws of the land that were later contorted to fit their desire for slavery.

Back to Governor Coles and the obstacles he faced from the pro-slavery legislation. The legislators believed that all slave owners had authority under the cessation deed of Virginia. They believed they had the right to call forth a convention. The purpose would be to alter the state of the constitution. This was important to people living in Illinois and for Governor Coles. He had to fight even harder for Illinois to pass a law to make Illinois a free state. There were more northeastern emigrants coming to Illinois. These were free state thinkers. This threatened the slave holders. They needed a law to keep their slaves.

Coles documents that were bequeathed to his son show that, "*The pro-slavery men were, as they have always been, ready to resort to violence wherever they dared, unwilling to listen to, or incapable of comprehending arguments. Their method of overcoming opposition was by 'bull dozing.'*" On the other hand, Coles and other anti-slavery people would have to stand up to these bully's with wit and confidence to defend their positions despite the hazards. Why? Many of these anti-slavery men came to Illinois to get rid of the curse of slavery.

A provision of the Illinois constitution stated that no change could be made unless the new constitution should be submitted to the people by a joint resolution of the legislature, adopted, by a two-thirds vote. While the pro-slavery men had precisely two-thirds of the votes of the Senate, in the House, they lacked one vote of the requisite number. Yes, one vote would pass the new constitution for a free state! During the next 18-months there was a political struggle. People on both sides used committees in each county to fight for their cause. They even used travelling preachers to promote a free state.

Reverend John Mason Peck helped Governor Coles by talking to people throughout southern Illinois. He educated them on the convention issue in Vandalia and its' political parties. Peck protected his biblical mission and showed no partisan party. It was interesting to note that men in authority did not always agree with Peck. He still had a way of softening the hardest of hearts. Within time, they would approach him and found him pleasant and non-judgmental. Peck wrote that pro-slavery advocates were fewer than when the law was introduced.

Thomas Lippincott was an anti-slavery citizen. He published some wrong information about Governor Coles. This was a decade after the vote. He said that Coles lacked enthusiasm during the voting period. He also said that Coles never wrote much in the local newspapers in those 18 months. Communication was done through letters in the mail, newspapers, and churches. Coles wrote him a letter with courtesy but corrected his wrong assumptions.

Coles stated that, *"The hostility imbibed by Mr. Warren against me prevented my contributing to his paper (The Edwardsville Spectator), but I contributed to other papers, over various signatures, and published several pamphlets, and caused many to be published, several of which I assisted in circulating, particularly those you allude to from the enlightened and philanthropic pen of my friend, Roberts Vaux, of this city (Philadelphia). My labor in the cause was so great that during the several months which passed between the purchasing the Illinois Intelligencer, there were but few numbers of that paper which did not contain some article from my pen, either original essays- the most methodical and lengthy of which were contained in nine numbers over the signature of 'One of Many'. Also, numerous extracts from the writings and speeches of the most celebrated men of America and Europe, many of which were published under the title of 'The Voice of Virtue - Wisdom and Experience on the Subject of Negro Slavery.'* [Signed] *Edward Coles."*

During Governor Coles time in office, the state was separated. There were heated discussions. There was more dissention over who would be replaced in the legislature for that one or two votes. The pro-slavery delegates were unscrupulous. The freedom loving delegates comprised the minority with conviction and dedication.

In summary, the Pro-slavery delegates called for a convention. They were sure that they would win. All their discouraging tactics did not work. Then they worried about getting a majority vote. They took an anti-convention man [anti-slavery] out and put a convention man [pro-slavery] in. This would insure the two-thirds vote to pass. The man they voted in as the pro-convention representative was Nicholas Hansen. At the last minute he voted against the convention. Anti-slavery won. On August 2, 1824, Illinois voters rejected the pro-slavery convention referendum. The convention was defeated and Illinois was voted in as a free state.

Coles concludes later in life that: "*I should like to expatiate on the great excitement and our consequent labors at the times of my election, and especially at the succeeding election two years afterwards to prevent Illinois from being made a slave holding state. The longer I live the more I see and hear of the disgraceful proceedings of the present day, the more pleasing the consolation I feel in reflecting on the efforts and agency I had in our successful labors in the cause of freedom, and against the curse of slavery and its extension over the lovely state of Illinois.*"

CHAPTER FIVE

Politicians File a Lawsuit Against
Governor Coles

Early in his college days, Edward Coles declared that "all men are born free and equal". He believed that the institution of slavery should not exist in a democracy. Thus, he decided that he would not own slaves nor live in a state that allowed slavery. He wrote to President Thomas Jefferson in 1814 the following: "*I have not only been principled against slavery, but have had feelings so repugnant to it* [slavery] *as to decide me not to hold them; which decision has forced me to leave my native State* [Virginia], *and with it all my relations and friends.*"

A lawsuit was filed in Edwardsville, Illinois against Coles in 1819. The states wanted to collect $200 for each slave that he freed and brought into Illinois. Coles was not aware that a law had passed in March 30, 1819. The law was not published until October 1819. Coles and his slaves came to Illinois during the first week of May 1819. This lawsuit was senseless and it caused Coles great grief.

Governor Coles was devastated with the unfairness of people that would attack him in this way. The law suit was full of legal language and sought to destroy Coles financially. Coles wrote to Morris Birkbeck, of Edwards County, on January 29, 1824 from Vandalia. He wrote about his financial responsibility when he brought his slaves to Illinois. He said that it cost one-third of all the property his father bequeathed to him to pay for their freedom. Then is cost him between $500-$600 to move them from Virginia to Illinois. He then gave each head of family and those over 24 years old, one hundred and sixty acres each. In return they were to be honest, industrious, and correct in conduct. They excelled at being good citizens so no one could find fault.

Coles was consoled by his correspondence with Birkbeck. He goes on to tell Birkbeck that he lost part of his farm due to a fire. He lost two-thirds of all his buildings and enclosures. He also lost 200 mature apple trees and as many mature peach trees. At about the same time, the State House at Vandalia had burned down. Coles did not like the way the third State House would be built. He told the convention how it should be paid. The pro-slavery or factious convention were not happy with him. They wanted to make the anti-slavery population or anti-conventions' pay for it. Governor Coles says it like this, " . . . *they* [factious conventions'] *busied themselves in misrepresenting to the multitude my reasons and motives for not subscribing my name to their paper, and with the aid of large portions of whiskey, contrived to get up a real vandal mob, who vented their spleen against me, in the most noisy and riotous manner, nearly all night, for my opposition to a convention and for my refusal as they termed it, to rebuild the State House.*"

This distressed Coles and he goes on to say that in his bosom he had feelings of pain and pleasure. On one hand, there was pain because of the vindictive nature of some people. Also, he was opposed to one people oppressing the other. His pleasure came from doing the right thing. He was in the right position for having done the right thing for the cause of anti-slavery. He concludes his letter giving thanks to Providence. His guidance let Coles get through the contest. He had the strength to endure the injustice that came with it.

Governor Coles continued corresponding with Birkbeck. Cole told him that the persecution continued. He felt that the enemy would not be satisfied until he was completely ruined. Coles told him that a trial had been called about freeing his slaves. Judge Reynolds [pro-slavery] cited several laws against Coles. Judge Reynolds and Mr. Turney rejected all Coles statements as illegal. Coles was left without a defense. The jury found a verdict of $2,000. This would be difficult to pay in those hard times.

Coles filed for an appeal to the Illinois Supreme Court. It did go to the Illinois Supreme Court and his case was argued and then adjourned. Eventually, the Supreme Court found Coles innocent of this malicious law suit.

CHAPTER SIX

*Elijah Lovejoy's Murder by the
Mob in Alton, Illinois*

Elijah Lovejoy's Printing Press Warehouse

Reverend Elijah Parish Lovejoy (1802 – 1837), was shot 5 times by a pro-slavery mob on November 7, 1837. This was 13 years after Illinois became a free state. The news made it to the east coast of America and everyone was talking about it. He was one of the first martyrs to die defending the ideals that every man was free. But as you can see, slavery was still being practiced. This was a blister or an open sore on mankind, on the United States Constitution, and on the Illinois law.

This story was told by Elijah's two brothers in a document with an introduction written by John Quincy Adams in 1838. His brothers said, Elijah Lovejoy had already lost three printing presses to the mob. His brothers, Joseph and Owen, wrote, " . . . *about the middle of October he* [Elijah] *sent for another press. Three, as will be recollected, had already been destroyed. One on his arrival, on the 21st of July, 1836, one on the 21st of August, 1837, and one on the 21st of September following. This last press he* [Elijah] *sent for on his own account, . . .* "

Elijah and his wife, Celia Ann Lovejoy, were terrified. The mob tormented them for three nights at home. Each time, they demanded his printing press. His brothers were present and tried to protect Elijah and his wife. By now, Mrs. Lovejoy would get startled when she heard any little noise. Elijah waited for the fourth printing press. The pro-slavery mob planned to throw it in the Mississippi River.

Elijah's resolve was to stay at Alton no matter the danger. But on the other hand, he thought it was a sinful waste to have the presses thrown into the Mississippi River. His friends were becoming indifferent. His enemies were vigilant so he felt the press should be relocated. Elijah had friends in Quincy that would protect his press. It might have been a move if Elijah didn't have enough friends in Alton.

Either of his brothers were with him all the time. Meanwhile, conventions and committees were calling together anti-slavery supporters. They discussed the delivery of the printing press to Alton. Many of Elijah's friends were writing to him suggesting that maybe now was not the time to move it. There were mobs waiting for it to arrive.

Elijah wrote a call to action in the Alton Observer newspaper. The insert read, "*This call spoke of the importance of the subject of Slavery, the impossibility of remaining idle spectators in a moral contest which was agitating our country, and requesting those 'who earnestly longed, and prayed for the immediate abolition of Slavery' to meet in Convention, for the benefit of mutual discussion and deliberation; not feeling themselves [pledged, word missing] thereby, to any definite mode of action.*" There were two hundred and fifty signatures from all parts of Illinois. Elijah Lovejoy printed straight forward language which agitated the mob. He was never shy about 'freedom of speech'. His cause was about anti-slavery and freedom of speech.

During the week that led up to the murder of Lovejoy, both sides had committees. The slavery supporters were becoming more violent and malicious. They also held charges against Lovejoy. They attacked not only abolitionists but they included religion and ministers, too. They declared that no religious paper would be tolerated.

Elijah stood up to the chairman of the pro-slavery committee and asked about what law he had violated. It resulted in a difficult discussion. Elijah knew that he answered to the fear of God and not to the fear of men. The pro-slavery committee said that he enjoyed the spectacle. He said that he did not enjoy opposing his fellow citizens [pro-slavery]. He did not derive delight from the excitement of a disturbance.

The mob was volatile and was waiting for the right moment to strike Lovejoy down. An observer remarked that Lovejoy and his friends were calm throughout the meeting. He went on to say that they prayed to God all day.

The printing press was expected any day. Finally, on Sunday night on the 5th of November the steamship arrived in St. Louis with the press. Only Elijah and a few men knew that it would be delivered on Tuesday morning in the dark. Mr. W. S. Gilman and Elijah Lovejoy went to Mayor John Krum of Alton to request constabulary to protect them. The mayor, alderman, clerk, and Common Council wrote a note to suggest taking a vote. The note also said that Lovejoy and his friends should not establish an abolitionist's press. They went home and left the note on a table and nothing was done about it.

Elijah Lovejoy's Printing Store

On Monday night, the mayor and approximately 50 citizens showed up at the warehouse of Godfrey, Gilman & Company. This was the place where the press was to be stored. They were to uphold the law armed with rifles and muskets, loaded with buckshot or small balls. They were ordered to shoot any mob that showed up. Lovejoy never showed up. At this time, the assaults on his home were nightly. Lovejoy and one brother would take turns with the other brother and would stand guard at home or at the store. Each night they would stay in a different place.

At Two O'clock on Tuesday morning, the press arrived without notice. There were sentinels from both sides stationed up and down the Mississippi River. The boat would stop at St. Louis and then deliver the press in Alton. It was getting late and the mayor did not have enough men left and he could not muster anymore men so nothing happened. During the day on Tuesday, everyone knew that the press was in the stone warehouse.

Taverns and coffee houses released their drunken citizens on Tuesday at Ten O'clock that night. A mob of 30 people made a line and armed themselves with stones, pistols, and guns. They demanded the press at the warehouse. Those inside were stationed at different parts of the building. Mr. Gilman, one of the owners of the store, asked what they wanted. The leader of the mob, Mr. William Carr, said they wanted the press. Mr. Gilman assured Mr. Carr that they wanted no trouble and did not want to harm anyone. The mob began a riot at the warehouse.

Stones were thrown which broke several windows. Those inside agreed not to shoot unless they were in danger. After some gunfire from the mob, both sides started firing at each other. At first, no one inside was hurt but one man outside was killed and several were hurt. Firing stopped and the mob picked up their wounded and one dead man. They left temporarily. Things only escalated when the men returned from the taverns. They brought ladders and intended to set the roof on fire. The mob called the mayor and Justice Robbins to offer a flag of truce to those inside. They told Lovejoy and those inside that they would not be harmed if they gave up the press. Mr. Gilman who was inside, said that they were there to protect their property and that is what they would do. The mayor said that Lovejoy and his friends had the right to protect themselves with arms. The mob was excited and started a fire on the roof. It was now near midnight.

The bells rung in Alton and many citizens came to watch the arson and murder under a full moon. They did nothing but watch. There were five men inside that went outside to protect their store from more fire. A few of Lovejoy's men shot at a man on a ladder and he ran away. This made the mob go away. Those five men returned inside the warehouse to re-load their guns.

Elijah Lovejoy, Mr. Weller, and a few others stepped outside the door. There were men from the mob hiding behind a stack of lumber. Lovejoy was exposed and he was shot. In the words of his brothers, *"Our brother received five balls, three in his breast, two on the left and one on the right side* [breast]*, one in the abdomen, and one in his left arm. He turned quickly round into the store, ran hastily up a flight of stairs, with his arms across his breast, came into the counting-room, and fell, exclaiming" Oh God, I am shot," "I am shot," and expired in a few moments."*

Reverend Harned went outside and informed the mob that Lovejoy had died. The men inside were willing to give up the press if they could go without harm. The mob was worked up and shouted that they would all find a grave inside the warehouse. Mr. West saw their dire situation. He shouted a warning that they should leave the building or the mob would destroy everything. The roof was on fire.

The Mob Broke the Press Into Pieces

The men inside the warehouse ran down the shore line and the mob shot at them. No one was injured. The rest of the mob broke the press into pieces and threw it out of the window. They broke a few guns as well. The fire on the roof was extinguished. They offered no dignity to Lovejoy who was laying on a cot, dead.

The story of Lovejoy's murder was a brutal one. You can see the hatred of the pro-slavery faction against the anti-slavery citizens. Lovejoy knew he might die and wrote a letter. He offered prayers to God. That if he were to die, this was a good cause. He wanted freedom of the press and to extinguish slavery for the rights of man. He was 35 years old.

Elijah Lovejoy's Monument in Alton, Illinois

CHAPTER SEVEN

Coles Retired in Pennsylvania

W e come to the end of Edward Coles story. He continued farming in Edwardsville. He formed Illinois' first agricultural society. On December 25, 1830, Coles was honored with a county named for him. It was a large and important county called Coles County. Coles did not have a family. He suffered from bad health and left Illinois in 1833 at 46 years old. He spent much of his time at his old home in Virginia. He still travelled to Washington, Philadelphia, New York, and Saratoga.

Mrs. Sally Coles

He moved to Philadelphia where he developed friendships among, ". . . *the most distinguished and cultivated people*". "*On the 28th of November, 1833, he was married by Bishop De Lancey to Miss Sally Logan Roberts, a daughter of Hugh Roberts, a descendant of Hugh Roberts, of Peullyn, Wales, who came to this country with William Penn, in 1682.*"

Edward Coles led a wonderful life in comfort with his wife. He was an affectionate husband, devoted father to three children, and a kind friend to all. Although he lived a private life, we do know that he kept his interest in public affairs. He continued correspondence with the leading men of his time.

He wrote a paper about the Ordinance of 1787. It was read before the Historical Society of Pennsylvania, on June 9, 1856. It was one of the most completely covered subjects of its time. He reported that Illinois wanted to be a slave state during the time he was governor. He said, "*I think that I shall meet with indulgence from the zeal I have always felt in the cause, for adding that it has ever since afforded me the most delightful and consoling reflections that the abuse I endured, the labor I performed, the anxiety I felt, were not without their reward; and to have it conceded by opponents as well as supporters, that I was chiefly instrumental in preventing a call of a Convention, and in making Illinois a Slave-holding State.*" He prevented the pro-slavery Convention from making Illinois a slave-holding state.

Edward Coles died at his home in Philadelphia after many years of ill health on July 7, 1868. Coles was 82 years old. His family interred his ashes at Woodlawn near Philadelphia. He was survived by his wife and two children. The couples third youngest child died in February 1862.

Edward Coles Monument, Edwardsville, Illinois

Governor Edward Coles ashes are not mixed with the soil in Illinois. His dedication, suffering, and voice for freedom will be with Illinois for eternity.

CHAPTER EIGHT

*Rev John Mason Peck's College
and Churches Today*

Reverend John Mason Peck

T here were some good grade schools but Illinois was still behind the other 20 states. Early Illinois had their fair share of educated preachers. It needed a way to educate future preachers from the state. Reverend John Mason Peck had a theological college in mind as early as 1817. After 1825 it became an obsession. Peck realized that Baptist members could not rise above their preachers. He went East to raise $500 in 1826. By early 1827, he began to build Rock Springs Seminary on his farm. His first attempt to secure a charter failed. There was an anti-mission preacher-legislator that cast the deciding vote against it. In 1832, the school was moved to Upper Alton. To prevent its closing, Peck went East in 1835 to raise funds. Benjamin Shurtleff, M.D., of Boston, donated $10,000. In 1836 the school was renamed Shurtleff College. It ceased operation in 1957. The current Southern Illinois University (SIU) campus in Edwardsville, Illinois opened in 1965. Portions of the Shurtleff campus became the SIU Dental School in 1972. It still exists today. In 1836, Peck became the secretary of the new Illinois Baptist Education Society. He was honored with a doctor of divinity degree from Harvard University.

First Baptist Church, 3100 Bell Ave, St. Louis, Misssouri

First Baptist Church of St. Louis, Missouri is the oldest extant black church. Its history dates back to 1817. Two Baptist missionaries; John Mason Peck, of Connecticut, and James E. Welch, of Kentucky arrived in St. Louis. They were sent by the Baptist Triennial Missionary Convention based in Philadelphia. Peck and Welch saw a need for a black church and helped to get them started. They became acquainted with a free black man named John Berry Meachum. Meachum would lead the black church in St. Louis. Peck started many black churches in his time.

Pastor John Berry Meachum

John Berry Meachum made remarkable achievements. He became the first pastor of First Baptist Church at 1 Memorial Drive in St. Louis. He defied the law which forbade African Americans from being educated. He taught free men by building a steamboat and anchoring it in the middle of the Mississippi River. The boat served as a school. It provided hundreds of African Americans with an education in the 1840s through the 1850s. Because the river was under federal jurisdiction, Meachum's school was within the law. One of Meachum's pupils was James Milton Turner, who went on to be America's first African American diplomat.

Under Meachum's leadership, the First Baptist Church started with 14 people. In two months that number increased to 100, ranging in age from 5 to 40 years. The church was located on Almond until 1885, when it relocated to a building on Clark Street. From Clark, the congregation moved to Bell, in a church that dates to 1882. First Baptist is currently located at 3100 Bell Ave., in a building it has occupied since 1920. It was designed by noted architect C. K. Ramsey. In 1942 the structure suffered a fire and was rebuilt.

Reverend Peck was instrumental in many ways. He encouraged education for the people of Illinois. He wrote a detailed gazetteer describing early Illinois' geography and resources. This book helped the emigrants make their home here. He traveled through Southern Illinois to educate people on the need to vote for anti-slavery. News was slow and he started his own newspaper. There were a few other preachers who helped early Illinois. Reverend Peck dedicated his whole life to furthering the state. He helped to remove the blight of slavery that cast a dark shadow on humanity. He was an unsung non-elected statesman. He used his educated mind in the Vandalia legislature. He made sure that every man had the inalienable right to be free.

Peck died on March 16, 1858, and he was buried in Bellefontaine Cemetery in St. Louis. Today, 2019, there is a cemetery located in O'Fallon, Illinois which used to be Rock Spring, Illinois in Peck's time. The O'Fallon Historical Society has reclaimed the old cemetery from ruin. It is now a respectful resting area for Peck's family, civil war soldiers, and early area residents. It is maintained by O'Fallon city with help from the historical society.

The sad story about Peck's burial was that he was exhumed 29 days after he was buried at Rock Spring cemetery. He was buried with other notable people from the area at Bellefontaine Cemetery. Mr. John Mason Peck and Mrs. Sally Peck [1789-1856)] were separated by the Mississippi River for 200 years. The O'Fallon Historical Society approached the city of O'Fallon to procure a beautiful memorial grave marker for Peck. It was paid for by the city of O'Fallon.

Pastor Reverend Henry L. Midgett and his wife, First Lady Jacqueline R. Midgett. Pastor of a 200 year old church found by Reverend John Mason Peck.

Saturday, September 30, 2017 at 2 pm, the public was invited to the dedication ceremony. The cenotaph was in memory of Rev. John Mason Peck at Rock Spring Cemetery in O'Fallon, Illinois. Remember the First Baptist Church in St. Louis noted above? Pastor Reverend Henry L. Midgett and his wife, First Lady Jacqueline R. Midgett were invited to bless the event. They were with several members of the First Baptist Church of St. Louis, 3100 Bell Avenue, St Louis, MO 63108. This Church Celebrated 200 years and was founded by Reverend John Mason Peck in 1817. The First Baptist Church of St Louis provided the Central Red Rose Wreath. The wreath was between the graves of Sarah Payne-Peck and Rev. John Mason Peck. Reverend Midgett was one of the Speakers and he gave the closing benediction. Brian Keller, O'Fallon Historical Society President and Thomas Marshall Schwarztrauber, RPh,

O'Fallon Historical Society Vice President were speakers for the dedication.

Peck's original home caught fire but you can see the replacement home from Highway 50. It is private property so no visitors are allowed. To the North of the house was where the seminary resided. To the Northeast of his home is where the cemetery rests. You can visit the Rock Spring Cemetery by travelling East on Route 50, (heading from O'Fallon to Lebanon) past the intersection at Scott-Troy Road. Travel one quarter mile on Route 50 and turn North at Commerce Drive. The cemetery is obscure but it can be found.

ACKNOWLEDGEMENTS

I owe a debt of gratitude to my friend and poet, Judy Huffman, for proofreading and friendship. She is an immense help to me when I can't see the forest for the trees. Judy offers me a cup of coffee and some reassurance. She helps me work through what I want to say.

CHRONOLOGY

Chapter Three

Timeline in Illinois slave history:

1817, in December, a campaign began for Illinois' admission to the Union.

1818, in December, Illinois becomes the 21st state. Adopted a constitution which prohibited slavery and involuntary servitude.

1,173 African Americans in the Illinois Territorial Census. There were 847 servants or slaves and 326 were free African Americans.

1819, future Illinois Governor Edward Coles (1822-1826) migrated from Virginia. He manumitted (set free) his slaves. He gave each family 160 acres of land in Illinois.

1820, 1,512 African Americans in the Illinois State Census. There were 668 slaves and 469 were free African Americans. About 375 African Americans had no designation.

1822-1824, the struggle to abolish slavery dominated politics in Illinois.

1822, on December 5, Governor Coles called for the legislature to abolish slavery.

1824, in March, Governor Coles was sued for manumitting his slaves. He was found guilty in the lower courts. Then sited as innocent by the Illinois Supreme Court.

1824, voters defeated a call for a constitutional convention. This abolished slavery.

Chapter Four

Edward Coles timeline as governor:

1787, Northwest Ordinance was made a law. Congress voted that the area west of Pennsylvania and north of the Ohio River would be slave-free.

1817, James Monroe becomes the President of the United States.

1819, Coles moved to Edwardsville, Illinois and manumitted his slaves.

1821, Missouri Compromise, sets 36' 30 as the demarcation between free and slave states.

1822, Edward Coles was inaugurated as the second governor of Illinois.

1823, the Illinois legislature passed a bill calling for a constitutional convention. Proponents of the convention supported legal protections for slave owners.

1823, a law suit was filed against Illinois Governor Edward Coles. It accused him of freeing his slaves without posting a necessary bond.

1824, Illinois Governor Edward Coles purchased the Illinois Intelligencer paper of Vandalia. It was used to promote the anti-slavery cause.

1824, Coles received a summons. He had to answer charges that he freed his slaves without posting a necessary bond.

1824, in Illinois, a statewide referendum defeats the call for a constitutional convention. This would have strengthened legal protections for slavery. Illinois was a free state.

1825, John Quincy Adams took the oath of office as President of the United States.

1826, the Supreme Court of Illinois ruled that Governor Edward Coles was innocent. There were no violations in the freeing of his slaves.

1826, Edward Coles finished his term as governor of Illinois.

1831, Coles moved from Illinois to Philadelphia, Pennsylvania.

1833, Coles announced that he would run for the U.S. Senate. He lost the election.

1863, Emancipation Proclamation abolished slavery. It allowed the enlistment of black servicemen in the Union army.

1864, Lincoln wins re-election.

1865, Congress passed the 13th Amendment abolishing slavery in the United States.

Chapter Five

Politicians File a Lawsuit against Governor Coles:

1823, politicians from Madison County, Illinois filed a lawsuit. It was against Illinois Governor Edward Coles. Accusing him of freeing his slaves without paying taxes on the bonds.

1824, Governor Edward Coles purchases the Illinois Intelligencer of Vandalia. Purpose was to promote the anti-slavery cause.

1824, Governor Coles received a summons. He was to answer charges that he freed his slaves without posting a necessary tax on the bonds.

1824, statewide referendum defeated the call for a constitutional convention. This likely would have strengthened legal protections for slavery.

1825, John Quincy Adams took the oath of office as President of the United States.

1826, The Supreme Court of Illinois rules in favor of Governor Edward Coles. He did not break the law on taxes.

Edward Coles Timeline

In Coles own words he said: *"I was born in Albemarle county, Virginia, on the 15th Dec. 1786. While at William and Mary College I imbibed the belief that man could not of right hold property in his fel-*

low man and under this conviction determined to remove the chain of
slavery and to emigrate to and reside with my colored people in one of
the new free states or territories."

1808-1809, Edward Coles inherits his father's land. It included 19 slaves most under age 30 years. He put the land up for sale the following year.

1812, the war with England kept him from selling his inherited land. The economy was struggling.

1810, President James Madison asked Edward Coles to be his personal secretary. This further retards Coles effort to sell his inherited land. It takes Coles six years to sell it.

1815, peace was made with England. Coles resigned from President Madison's secretary-ship. He explored a slave free state in the western country to find a permanent home in Ohio, Indiana, or Illinois.

1815, the Indians in Illinois are still hostile. Coles first visit to Illinois in October. He traveled into Illinois by Kaskaskia. Then moved north through the state to avoid any residual problems with Indians from the War of 1812.

1815, Coles visits Edwardsville where he would settle in 1819.

1816, President Madison implores Edward Coles to travel on special business to Russia. He finished the diplomatic business in Russia. Then spent one year in Europe on personal time.

1817, Coles returned to America. He spends time with his 'relations' and embarks for Illinois.

1818, Coles explored the Illinois country. This is his second appearance in Illinois at Kaskaskia.

1818, Illinois becomes the 21st state.

1819, Coles slaves were manumitted.

1819, President James Monroe appointed Coles as Receiver of the Land Office at Edwardsville. He held that position until he was elected governor of Illinois.

1822, Governor Edward Coles was elected the second governor of Illinois.

1823, while Coles served as governor at the Vandalia Capital. His farm burned to the ground in a prairie fire.

1823, the same year the Vandalia State House burned down.

1824, legislation passed banning slavery.

1826, his term as governor of Illinois ended.

1833, Coles lost his race for senator.

1833, Coles left Illinois at age 46 and moved to Pennsylvania and married Sally Logan Roberts.

NOTES

CHAPTER ONE

Carveth, B. G. Edward Coles (1786–1868). (2014, July 17). In Encyclopedia Virginia. Retrieved from http://www.EncyclopediaVirginia.org/Coles_Edward_1786-1868. Accessed January 21, 2019.

Blumrose, Alfred; Blumrose, Ruth, Slave Nation: How Slavery United the Colonies And Sparked The American Revolution, Sourcebooks Inc (February 28, 2005), pp. 246-8.

Carveth, p. 59.

Washburne, E. B., *Sketch of Edward Coles, second governor of Illinois, and of the slavery, struggle of 1823-4*, Prepared for the Chicago historical society. Pp. 49-52.

NOTE: Honorable E. B. Washburne was given Governor Edward Coles documents by his son, Edward Coles, Esq., of Philadelphia to write this Sketch. The Chicago Historical Society voted to have Honorable E. B. Washburne who lived in Illinois 40 years and was a respectable historian to his peers, to write the *"Sketch of Edward Coles"*. Although Washburne finds these papers interesting, he feels that he cannot connect an accurate story without most of the files that were burned in a house fire of Rev. Peck. But he promises to do his best.

CHAPTER TWO

Coles, Edward. *"Governor Coles' Autobiography: Letter from Governor Edward Coles to the Late Senator W. C. Flagg: Early Settlements in Madison County."*Journal of the Illinois State Historical Society (1908-1984), vol. 3, no. 3, 1910, pp. 59–64. JSTOR, http://www.jstor.org/stable/40193772, pp. 62-64. Accessed February 3, 2019.

Peck, John Mason, 1789-1858. [from old catalog]. A Gazetteer of Illinois, In Three Parts. 2d ed. Philadelphia: Grigg & Elliott, 1837. Pp. 116-7, 181-2, 194.

CHAPTER THREE

Reynolds, John, My own times: embracing also the history of my life . . . , Printed by B. H. Perryman and H. L. Davison, Illinois 1855, p.230.

Ekberg, Carl J., French Roots in the Illinois Country: the Mississippi Frontier in Colonial Times. Urbana: University of Illinois Press, 1998. P. 146

Washburne, p. 63.

CHAPTER FOUR

Note: Illinois had five capitals. First capital was at Kaskaskia, Illinois, fell into the meandering Mississippi River. Second capital or State House, Vandalia, Illinois, where Governor Coles worked, burned down. Third State House was at Vandalia, Illinois and still exists. Fourth Capital, Springfield, Illinois, Fifth Capital, the current one in 2019, Springfield, Illinois.

Washburne, pp.61, 67, 71.

Babcock, Rufus, Memoir of John Mason Peck, Forty Years of Pioneer Life, Southern Illinois University Press, 1965, p. 195.

"Edward Coles, Second Governor of Illinois: Correspondence with Rev. Thomas Lippincott." Journal of the Illinois State Historical Society (1908-1984), vol. 3, no. 4, 1911, pp. 59–63. http://www.jstor.org/stable/40193544.

NOTE: Edward Coles Correspondence with Rev. Thomas Lippincott. These letters were Edward Coles' rebuttals to Rev. Lippincott for publishing wrong information about him years later. Coles replies to Lippincott's letters saying, *"There is among the vol-*

umes loaned, a file of the Illinois Intelligencer from I think soon after the establishment of the Illinois Territory, to about the year 1834 bound in volumes. It may also be of service for me here to add that I gave to the library of the Secretary of State a volume of the Edwardsville Spectator, which included the four years I served as Governor. Those files of newspapers, especially the last from its having been printed in the county, must contain much that is of interest about Madison. At the request of Josiah Meigs, then commissioner of the Coles letters to Flagg. Edward Coles". He also tells Lippincott that the bulk of his archives were burned in a fire.

Coles, Edward, pp. 63-64.

https://www2.illinois.gov/dnrhistoric/Research/Pages/GenPrideAfAm.aspx, A Selected Chronology by Kathryn M. Harris, Illinois Department of Natural Resources Historic Preservation Division, accessed February 3, 2019.

Blumrose, p. 225.

CHAPTER FIVE

Washburne, p. 24.

The Journal of Negro History, edited by Carter Godwin Woodson, published Washington D. C., Vol IV, No.1, January 1921. P. 182.

CHAPTER SIX

Lovejoy, Joseph C., Lovejoy, Owen, *Memoir of the Rev. Elijah P. Lovejoy: Who Was Murdered in Defense of the Liberty of the Press*, at Alton, Illinois, New York, Nov. 7, 1837. Pp. 261, 264, 291.

CHAPTER SEVEN

Washburne, pp. 16, 246, 248.

CHAPTER EIGHT

http://www.sbhla.org/bio_peck.htm. From the Special Collections of the St. Louis Mercantile Library at the University of Missouri – St. Louis.

Keller, Brian, President, O'Fallon Historical Society, Ceremony

Brochure, September 30, 2017.

EDWARD COLES TIMELINE (Chronology)

Governor Coles' Autobiography: Letter from Governor Edward Coles to the Late Senator W. C. Flagg: Early Settlements in Madison County" is an article from Journal of the Illinois State Historical Society (1908-1984), Volume 3, p.64, http://www.jstor.org/stable/10.2307/40193772, Accessed 20 January 2019.

Note: The content of this book was written and quoted from *Governor Coles Autobiography* by Flagg and the *Sketch of Edward Coles* by Washburne. Flagg's documentation was written in 1861 approximately 35 years after being the governor of Illinois. The Honorable [Senator] W. C. Flagg, Esq., Moro, Madison county, Illinois collected the history of the early settlement of Madison County. Many of Coles carefully collected source documents were burned. There was a fire at Reverend John Mason Peck's house. Peck borrowed the documents to write the Illinois history. When he was finished, they were to be archived at the Alton Historical Society. Coles was an honorary member at Alton. Coles apologized for the fire and continued his account from memory. After Coles died, he bequeathed his letters as governor to his son who gave them to E. B. Washburne to do a sketch on Coles life.

GLOSSARY

American Bottom, the flood plain of the Mississippi River extending from Alton, Illinois to the south to the Kaskaskia River. It is also sometimes called "American Bottoms". The area is about 175 square miles. Mostly protected from flooding in the 21st century by a levee and drainage canal system. The Mississippi River forms the boundary to its west. The river boundary forms the bluff line on the Illinois side. There are industrial and urban areas and many swamps today. But when we look back to the early settler's, they used the rich alluvial (rich river sediment) floodplain mostly for agriculture until the late 19th century. Horseshoe Lake is a reminder of the Bottoms' riparian nature. (A riparian buffer or stream buffer is a vegetated area or a "buffer strip" near a stream, usually forested, which helps shade and partially protects the stream from the impact of adjacent land uses.) Looking at the American Bottom from Edward Coles point of view in 1815, it was the most precious land for growing crops and using wood. The river did not have levy's and the natural lay of the river was rich with flora and fauna. It had a natural barrier from the river. Portions of St. Clair, Madison, Monroe, and Randolph counties are in the American Bottom. The major cities include Alton, Granite City, Madison, Cahokia, and East St. Louis. Brooklyn, Illinois was founded in 1839 as a freedom village by free people of color and fugitive slaves, led by "Mother" Priscilla Baltimore. It was the first town incorporated by African Americans under a state legal system. Cha-Jua, Sundiata Keita (2000). *America's First Black Town: Brooklyn, Illinois, 1830-1915*, Urbana, IL: University of Illinois Press, 2002, p.85. https://drloihjournal.blogspot.com/2016/11/the-story-of-american-bottom-in-illinois.html

Brickbat (plural brickbats) A piece of broken brick used as a weapon when placed in something like a sock and used as a club.

Extant church, in existence, still existing not destroyed or lost.

Federalist: a member of a major political party in the early years of the U.S. favoring a strong centralized national government. Patterned after England. The New England states favored this pattern because they tended to trade with England when few states did.

Manumission, or enfranchisement, is the act of an owner freeing his or her slaves. Jamaican historian Verene Shepherd states that the most widely used term is gratuitous manumission, "the conferment of freedom on the enslaved by enslavers before the end of the slave system".

Primary source, if you are seeking to learn about the past, primary sources of information are those that provide first-hand accounts of the events, practices, or conditions you are researching. In general, these are documents that were created by the witnesses or first recorders of these events at about the time they occurred, and include diaries, letters, reports, photographs, creative works, financial records, memos, and newspaper articles (to name a few types).

Republican, of, relating to, or constituting the one of the two major political parties evolving in the U.S. in the mid-19th century that is usually primarily associated with business, financial, and some agricultural interests and is held to favor a restricted governmental role in economic life. This is not the Republicans we know today.

The Enlightenment, a philosophical movement of the 18th century marked by a rejection of traditional social, religious, and political ideas and an emphasis on rationalism. Early Presidents of the United States were an example of this. No long did a person have to come from nobility but they could educate themselves and make a fortune.

Webster, www.merriam-webster.com/

BIBLIOGRAPHY

Books

Babcock, Rufus, *Peck, John Mason, 1789-1858, and Forty Years of Pioneer Life: Memoir of John Mason Peck D.D.*, Philadelphia: American Baptist Publication Society, 1864.

Blumrose, Alfred; Blumrose, Ruth, *Slave Nation: How Slavery United the Colonies and Sparked The American Revolution*, Sourcebooks Inc (February 28, 2005), pp. 246-8.

Carveth, Bruce; Leichtle, Kurt; *Crusade against slavery: Edward Coles, pioneer of freedom*, Southern Illinois University Press, 2011.

Cooper, Suzanne, *Edward Coles and the Rise of Antislavery Politics in the Nineteenth Century America*, Northern Illinois University Press, 2013.

Ekberg, Carl J., *French Roots in the Illinois Country: the Mississippi Frontier in Colonial Times*. Urbana: University of Illinois Press, 1998. P. 146

Harris, Norman Dwight, *The History of Negro Servitude in Illinois 1719-1864*, A. C. McClurg & Co. Publisher, 1904.

Hayne, Coe. *Vangard of the caravans: a life story of John Mason Peck*, The Judson Press, 1931.

Lovejoy, Joseph C., Lovejoy, Owen, *Memoir of the Rev. Elijah P. Lovejoy: Who Was Murdered in Defense of the Liberty of the Press, at Alton, Illinois*, New York, Nov. 7, 1837, P, 261.

Reynolds, John, *My own times, embracing also the history of my life*, B. H. Perryman and H. L. Davison, 1855, https://archive.org/

details/myowntimesembrac00reyn.

Articles

Coles, Edward, *History of the Ordinance of 1787. Philadelphia*, Press of the Society, 1856.

Keller, Brian, President, O'Fallon Historical Society, Ceremony Brochure, September 30, 2017.

Kinton '61, Jack F., "Basic Issues of the Illinois Territory (1809-1818)" (1961). Honors Projects. Paper 43, http://digitalcommons.iwu.edu/history_honproj/43, 1961.

Moore , Gwen, *A Brief History of First Baptist Church*, https://mohistory.org/blog/a-brief-history-of-first-baptist-church/ April 26, 2011.

http://www.sbhla.org/bio_peck.htm. From the Special Collections of the St. Louis Mercantile Library at the University of Missouri – St. Louis.

Journals

Coles, Edward. *"Governor Coles' Autobiography: Letter from Governor Edward Coles to the Late Senator W. C. Flagg: Early Settlements in Madison County."*Journal of the Illinois State Historical Society (1908-1984), vol. 3, no. 3, 1910, pp. 59–64. JSTOR, http://www.jstor.org/stable/40193772, pp. 63-64. Accessed February 3, 2019.

"Edward Coles, Second Governor of Illinois: Correspondence with Rev. Thomas Lippincott." Journal of the Illinois State Historical Society (1908-1984), vol. 3, no. 4, 1911, pp. 59–63. http://www.jstor.org/stable/40193544

"Front Matter." Journal of the Illinois State Historical Society (1908-1984), vol. 3, no. 4, 1911, JSTOR, www.jstor.org/stable/40193540. pp. 59-63, accessed February 1, 2019.

Journal of John Mason Peck, 1854-1856. MF 738, http://www.sbhla.org/bio_peck.htm.

Lawrence, Matthew, *John Mason Peck, the pioneer missionary: a biographical sketch, 1940*, Journal of Illinois History, Volume 15, Illinois Historic Preservation Agency, 2012.

President George Milion Potter, of Shurtleff College, & Castle, L. (1927). *Shurtleff College Centennial.* Journal of the Illinois State Historical Society (1908-1984), 20(2), 258-264. Retrieved from http://www.jstor.org/stable/40186914, accessed February 1, 2019.

Stevens, Wayne E. "*The Shaw-Hansen Election Contest: An Episode of the Slavery Contest in Illinois.*" Journal of the Illinois State Historical Society (1908-1984), vol. 7, no. 4, 1915, pp. 389–401. JSTOR, www.jstor.org/stable/40194443, Accessed February 1, 2019.

The Journal of Negro History, edited by Carter Godwin Woodson, published Washington D. C., Vol IV, No.1, January 1921. P. 182.

Washburne, E. B., *Sketch of Edward Coles, second governor of Illinois, and of the slavery, struggle of 1823-4*, Prepared for the Chicago historical society. Pp. 45-52.

Websites

https://www2.illinois.gov/dnrhistoric/Research/Pages/GenPrideAfAm.aspx, A Selected Chronology by Kathryn M. Harris, Illinois Department of Natural Resources Historic Preservation Division, accessed February 3, 2019.

Robinson, J. Eric, *Pin Oak Colony*, Edwardsville, IL., https://www.lib.niu.edu/1999/iht0619941.html and https://www.cityofedwardsville.com/327/Historic-Edwardsville

NOTE: There were books and articles that were not recommended because they lacked footnotes or sources.

PHOTO CREDITS

Coles, Edward, portrait, https://www.cyberdriveillinois.com/departments/library/heritage_project/home/chapters/the-birth-of-the-illinois-state-library/edward-coles/

Coles, Edward, Young, Darlington Digital Library, University of Pittsburgh, date unknown.

Coles, Edward, "Future Governor Edward Coles Freeing His Slaves While in route to Illinois 1819". Painting at the Illinois State Capital First Floor Rotunda, South Hall, Original Author: Phillips Decorative Company of Chicago, Created: 1885, Medium: Mural.

Edward Coles Memorial at Valley View Cemetery, Edwardsville, IL. Photo by Mary D. Hébert.

John Henry Brown (Painter), Portrait of Sally Logan Roberts Coles (Mrs. Edward Coles Sr.), 1855 and 1856, [Article] Verplanck, Anne. 11//2004 The Art of John Henry Brown. Antiques. 166 (5): 138-43. Published as pl. III, pp. 139 & 141-2.

1818 Statehood Map, Abraham Lincoln Presidential Library and Museum, Illinois, pre-Chicago, There are only four surviving copies of this 1818 map of Illinois, which was printed in Philadelphia. John Melish produced it from surveys in the General Land Office and a few other sources. Produced only a few months before Illinois achieved statehood, the map reflects the priorities of early settlement, highlighting military bounty lands granted to War of 1812 veterans. Note, too, that the northern border does not yet reach Lake Michigan. This conformed to the original statehood bill placed before Congress, but Illinois' Congressional delegate, Nathaniel Pope, quickly moved for an amendment to extend the border about sixty miles further north. Pope wanted to ensure his new state included ample room for a port city (what would become Chicago) and access to the lead mines around modern Galena. Congress approved, although debate with Wisconsin over the border continued well into the 1840s.

Lovejoy's Photographs

Courtesy of the Missouri History Museum.

Peck's Photographs

Courtesy of the St. Louis Mercantile Library Association, University of Missouri at St. louis.

ABOUT THE AUTHOR

Mary D. Hébert was an active duty United States Air Force Historian during the post-Vietnam and Gulf War eras. She holds a BA in History from the University of Nebraska. She wrote numerous Air Force proprietary history books over the course of her career and she is a member of her local Illinois historical society. She retired in Illinois and calls Southern Illinois her home for thirty years.

Made in the USA
Lexington, KY
12 May 2019